# JIM ALEXANDER

## Great Rides In California

*California has everything from rugged Coastline to
towering Sierra Nevada Mountians*

# Contents

# 1

# Introduction

Welcome to the 100 top Motorcycle rides in California. I am Jim Alexander; I have been the State Director for the Motorcycle Sport Touring in Califonia for 5 years in the past and have compiled these rides from my experience in riding in California. Please find these rides and enjoy them as I have! I have a passion for riding and have enjoyed all of these rides in the past 25 years in California.

This region is a true paradise for riders, with its breathtaking scenery, winding roads, and diverse landscapes. California has everything from the rugged coastline to the towering Sierra Nevada mountains. Whether you're looking for an adrenaline-pumping adventure or a leisurely ride through wine country, there is something here for every rider.

But with so many incredible routes to choose from, it can be overwhelming to know where to start. That's where this guide comes in. We have scoured California to bring you the best motorcycle routes and hidden gems this great region offers. So buckle up (or, instead, strap on your helmet), and get ready to hit the road.

The first thing we need to clear up is that I am not a lawyer, but I know these are the current laws in effect at the time of this book's writing. The first thing we need to clear up is that I am not a lawyer, but I know these are the current laws in effect at the time of this book's writing.

# 2

# California Motorcycle Laws

Before hitting the road on a motorcycle in California, it is vital to understand the state's laws regarding motorcycle operations. First and foremost, all riders must wear a helmet that meets state safety standards. The helmet must also have a DOT (Department of Transportation) sticker indicating that it meets federal safety standards.

In addition to helmet laws, riders must be aware of several other California motorcycle laws. For example, lane splitting is legal in California, meaning that motorcycles can ride between lanes of stopped or slow-moving traffic. However, riders must do so safely and prudently and cannot exceed the speed limit. This practice can be controversial, but it is essential to motorcycle riding in California.

Another important law to be aware of is California's requirement for motorcycle insurance. All riders must carry liability insurance with minimum coverage of $15,000 for bodily injury to one person, $30,000 for bodily injury to two or more people, and $5,000 for property damage. Failure to carry insurance can result in fines, suspension of your license, or even impoundment of your motorcycle.

4

# 3

# Motorcycle Safety in California

While California has some of the most scenic motorcycle routes in the world, it is also one of the most dangerous states for motorcycle riders. In 2019, there were over 5,000 motorcycle accidents in California, resulting in over 400 fatalities. To ensure your safety while riding in California, it is essential to take certain precautions.

First and foremost, always wear appropriate safety gear, including a DOT-approved helmet, motorcycle boots, gloves, and a jacket. Wearing bright or reflective clothing can also help increase your visibility to other drivers.

In addition to safety gear, riding defensively and anticipating potential hazards on the road is essential. This includes staying aware of your surroundings, maintaining a safe following distance, and being cautious when lane splitting. Always obey traffic laws and never ride under the influence of drugs or alcohol.

4

# Best California Motorcycle Routes

Riding a motorcycle in California can be an incredible experience despite the risks. Here are the Most Favorite motorcycle routes to take in the state. Enjoy the rides

## In the Northern California Area

o**Pacific Coast Highway**: The Pacific Coast Highway is one of the most iconic motorcycle routes in the world. This route takes riders along the California coast, offering breathtaking ocean views and the rugged coastline. The road stretches from San Francisco to San Diego, and there are numerous scenic stops along the way.

o**Yosemite National Park:** Yosemite National Park is one of the most beautiful places in the world and riding a motorcycle through the park is an unforgettable experience. The park features numerous scenic routes, including Tioga Road, which takes riders through the heart of the park and offers stunning views of the surrounding mountains and valleys.

o**Big Sur:** The Big Sur region of California is home to some of the most scenic motorcycle routes in the state. The way takes riders through winding roads along the coast, offering stunning views of the Pacific Ocean and the rugged coastline. The route is also home to several state parks and beaches, making it an excellent destination for a weekend trip..

o**Mount Hamilton:** Mount Hamilton is a popular motorcycle destination in Northern California. The road features several twists and turns and steep climbs and descents, making it a challenging but rewarding ride. The route also offers stunning views of the surrounding mountains and valleys.

o**Lake Tahoe:** Lake Tahoe is a popular destination for outdoor enthusiasts and an excellent place for motorcycle riding. The road around the lake offers stunning views of the lake and the surrounding mountains. There are also several scenic stops along the way, including Emerald Bay State Park and Sand Harbor.

o**Napa Valley:** Napa Valley is famous for its wineries and vineyards and is an excellent destination for motorcycle riding. The road through the valley offers stunning views of the surrounding hills and vineyards, and there are several stops along the way for wine tasting and sightseeing.

o **Redwood Highway:** The Redwood Highway takes riders through the majestic redwood forests of Northern California. The road winds through the woods, offering stunning views of the towering trees and the surrounding landscape. The route also passes through several small towns and coastal communities, making it an excellent multi-day trip.

o **Route 1:** Route 1, also known as the Pacific Coast Highway, is one of the most iconic motorcycle routes in the world. The route takes riders along the California coast, offering breathtaking ocean views and the rugged coastline. The road features numerous twists and turns and steep climbs and descents, making it a challenging but rewarding ride.

o **San Francisco to Lake Tahoe:** This route takes riders from the bustling city of San Francisco to the serene beauty of Lake Tahoe. The road winds through the Sierra Nevada Mountains, offering stunning views of the surrounding forests and mountains. Lake Tahoe is known for its crystal-clear waters, making it an excellent destination for a post-ride swim.

o **Gold Country:** The Gold Country region of California is known for its rich history and stunning scenery. The road winds through the foothills of the Sierra Nevada Mountains, offering spectacular views of the surrounding hills and valleys. The route also passes through several historic towns, including Sutter Creek and Nevada City, making it an excellent destination for a weekend trip.

o **Shasta Cascade:** The Shasta Cascade region of California is known for its stunning waterfalls, rivers, and lakes. The route takes riders through breathtaking views of the The road winds through the high desert and offers stunning views of the Sierra Nevada Mountains. The route also passes through several small towns, including Bishop and Lone Pine.

o **Route 299:** Route 299 is a popular motorcycle route that takes riders through Northern California's mountains and forests. Surrounding mountains and forests. The route is over 140 miles long and features several twists and turns that are sure to thrill even the most experienced riders. The road also passes through several small towns, including Redding and Weaverville. The route also passes through several small towns and historic sites, including the Lassen Volcanic National Park.

o **Lake County:** Lake County is home to several scenic

motorcycle routes that offer stunning views of the surrounding mountains and lakes. The road winds through the county's forests and hills, offering breathtaking views of Clear Lake and the surrounding valleys. The route also passes through several small towns, including Kelseyville and Lakeport.

o **Trinity Alps:** The Trinity Alps region of California offers some of the most stunning motorcycle routes in the state. The road winds through the Trinity Mountains, offering breathtaking views of the surrounding forests, rivers, and lakes. The route also passes through several small towns, including Weaverville and Trinity Center.

o **San Francisco to Yosemite:** This route takes riders from the bustling city of San Francisco to the stunning beauty of Yosemite National Park. The road winds through the Sierra Nevada Mountains, offering spectacular views of the surrounding forests and mountains. Yosemite National Park is known for its majestic waterfalls and granite cliffs, making it an excellent destination for a multi-day trip..

o **North Coast:** The North Coast of California is home to several scenic motorcycle routes that offer stunning views of the ocean and the coastline. The route takes riders through winding roads that pass through several charming coastal towns, including Fort Bragg and Mendocino. The route also passes through several state parks, including the Redwood National and State Parks.

o **Lassen Volcanic National Park:** Lassen Volcanic National Park is a popular destination for motorcycle riders, offering several scenic routes through the park's unique landscape. The road winds through the park's mountains and forests, offering stunning views of the surrounding valleys and lakes. The Park is also home to several volcanoes, making it an excellent destination for those interested in geology.

o **Sacramento River Delta:** The Sacramento River Delta is a popular destination for motorcycle riders, offering several scenic routes through the delta's unique landscape. The road winds through the delta's waterways, offering stunning views of the surrounding farmland and wetlands. The route also passes through several small towns, including Isleton and Rio Vista.

o **Monterey to Carmel:** This route takes riders along the stunning coastline of Monterey Bay, offering breathtaking views of the ocean and the rugged coastline. The road winds through the hills above the coastline, offering stunning views of the surrounding mountains and valleys. The route also passes through several charming coastal towns, including Pacific Grove and Carmel-by-the-Sea.

o **Sierra Buttes:** The Sierra Buttes region of California offers some of the most stunning motorcycle routes in the state. The road winds through the Sierra Buttes, offering breathtaking views of the surrounding forests and mountains. The route also passes through several small towns, including Downieville and Sierra City.

o **Sierra Nevada Mountains:** The Sierra Nevada Mountains offer several scenic motorcycle routes with stunning views of the surrounding mountains and forests. The Tioga Pass Road is a popular route that takes riders through Yosemite National Park, offering breathtaking views of the park's waterfalls and granite cliffs. The Sonora Pass Road is another popular route that winds through the Sierra Nevada Mountains, offering stunning views of the surrounding valleys and lakes.

o **Nacimiento-Fergusson Road:** The Nacimiento-Fergusson Road is a popular motorcycle route that takes riders through the Santa Lucia Mountains. The road features several twists and turns and steep climbs and descents, making it a challenging but rewarding ride. The route also offers stunning views of the surrounding forests and coastline.

o **Wine Country:** California's wine country is a popular destination for motorcycle riders, offering several scenic routes through the region's picturesque vineyards and wineries. The Silverado Trail is a popular route that winds through the Napa Valley, offering stunning views of the surrounding hills and vineyards. The Carmel Valley Road is another popular route that takes riders through the region's rolling hills and forests, offering breathtaking views of the surrounding landscapes.

o **Yosemite to Lake Tahoe:** This route takes riders from the stunning beauty of Yosemite National Park to the serene surroundings of Lake Tahoe. The road winds through the Sierra Nevada Mountains, offering spectacular views of the surrounding forests and mountains. Lake Tahoe is known for its crystal-clear waters, making it an excellent destination for a post-ride swim.

o **Tuolumne road to Twain Heart:** Tuolumne Road north towards Tuolumne City, then turn right onto Tuolumne Road North, passing through the small towns of Soulsbyville and Phoenix Lake. Take a left onto Longeway Road and follow it to the town of Twain Harte. Another option is to continue past Twain Harte to Pinecrest Lake. Overall, the Tuolumne Road to Twain Harte route is an excellent option for motorcycle enthusiasts looking to explore the scenic beauty of the Sierra Nevada Mountains

o **Route 1 to Half Moon Bay:** This route takes riders along the stunning coastline of California, offering breathtaking views of the ocean and the rugged coastline. The road winds through the hills above the coastline, offering stunning views of the surrounding mountains and valleys. Half Moon Bay is known for its charming downtown area and pristine beaches.

o **Point Reyes National Seashore:** Point Reyes National Seashore is a popular destination for motorcycle riders, offering several scenic routes through the park's unique landscape. The road winds through the park's forests and offers stunning views of the coastline and cliffs. The route also passes through several small towns, including Inverness and Olema.

o **Russian River:** The Russian River region of California is home to several scenic motorcycle routes that offer stunning views of the surrounding forests and rivers. The road winds through the region's hills and valleys, offering breathtaking views of the river and the surrounding landscapes. The route also passes through several small towns, including Guerneville and Monte Rio.

o **Mount Shasta:** Mount Shasta is a popular destination for motorcycle riders, offering several scenic routes through the surrounding mountains and forests. The road winds through the mountains and offers stunning views of the surrounding valleys and lakes. The route also passes through several small towns, including Weed and McCloud.

o **Trinity Alps:** The Trinity Alps region of California offers several scenic motorcycle routes that provide stunning views of the surrounding mountains and forests. The road winds through the region's hills and valleys, offering breathtaking views of the Trinity River and the surrounding landscapes. The route also passes through several small towns, including Weaverville and Junction City.

o **Shasta Lake:** Shasta Lake is a popular destination for motorcycle riders, offering several scenic routes through the surrounding mountains and forests. The road winds through the mountains and offers stunning views of the surrounding valleys and lakes. Shasta Lake is known for its crystal-clear waters, making it an excellent destination for a post-ride swim.

o **Route 36:** Route 36 is a popular motorcycle route that takes riders through Northern California's mountains and forests. The route is over 140 miles long and features several twists and turns that will thrill even the most experienced riders. The road also passes through several small towns, including Red Bluff and Fortuna.

o **Sierra Valley:** The Sierra Valley region of California offers several scenic motorcycle routes that offer stunning views of the surrounding mountains and valleys. The road winds through the region's hills and valleys, offering breathtaking views of the surrounding landscapes. The route also passes through several small towns, including Loyalton and Sierraville.

o **Avenue of the Giants:** The Avenue of the Giants is a popular motorcycle route that takes riders through the heart of the Redwood Forest. The road winds through the forest and offers stunning views of the surrounding giant redwood trees. The route also passes through several state parks, including Humboldt Redwoods State Park and Richardson Grove State Park.

o **San Francisco to Napa Valley:** This route takes riders from the bustling city of San Francisco to the serene surroundings of Napa Valley. The road winds through the hills above the town, offering stunning views of the surrounding landscape. Napa Valley is known for its vineyards and wineries, making it an excellent destination for wine lovers.

o **Mount Baldy:** Mount Baldy is a popular destination for motorcycle riders, offering several scenic routes through the mountain's unique landscape. The road winds through the mountain's forests and offers stunning views of the surrounding valleys and mountains. The route also passes through several small towns, including Claremont and Upland.

o **Route 108:** Route 108 is a popular motorcycle route that takes riders through the Sierra Nevada Mountains. The road features numerous twists and turns and steep climbs and descents, making it a challenging but rewarding ride. The route also offers stunning views of the surrounding mountains and valleys.

o **Lassen Volcanic National Park:** Lassen Volcanic National Park is a popular destination for motorcycle riders, offering several scenic routes through the park's unique landscape. The road winds through the park's mountains and offers stunning views of the surrounding volcanic features, including Lassen Peak and Bumpass Hell. The route also passes through several small towns, including Mineral and Chester.

o **Calaveras County:** Calaveras County is home to several scenic motorcycle routes that offer stunning views of the surrounding forests and mountains. The road winds through the county's hills and valleys, offering breathtaking views of the surrounding landscapes. The route also passes through several small towns, including Murphys and Angels Camp.

o **Lassen National Forest:** Lassen National Forest is a popular destination for motorcycle riders, offering several scenic routes through the forest's unique landscape. The road winds through the woods and offers stunning views of the surrounding mountains and valleys. The route also passes through several small towns, including Shingletown and Mineral.

o **Lake Tahoe:** Lake Tahoe is a popular destination for motorcycle riders, offering several scenic routes through the Sierra

Nevada Mountains. The road winds through the mountains and offers stunning views of the surrounding valleys and the clear blue waters of Lake Tahoe. The route also passes through several small towns, including South Lake Tahoe and Tahoe City.

o **Sequoia National Forest:** Sequoia National Forest is a popular destination for motorcycle riders, offering several scenic routes through the forest's unique landscape. The road winds through the woods and offers stunning views of the surrounding mountains and valleys. The route also passes through several small towns, including Kernville and Springville.

o **Mount Diablo:** Mount Diablo is a popular destination for motorcycle riders, offering several scenic routes through the mountain's unique landscape. The road winds through the mountain's forests and offers stunning views of the surrounding valleys and the city of San Francisco. The route also passes through several small towns, including Walnut Creek and Clayton.

o **Russian River to Mendocino:** This route takes riders through Northern California's stunning forests and coastline. The road winds through the hills and valleys and offers breathtaking views of the Russian River and the surrounding landscape. Mendocino is known for its charming downtown area and stunning coastline.

o **Sonoma County:** Sonoma County is home to several scenic motorcycle routes that offer stunning views of the surrounding vineyards and forests. The road winds through the county's hills and valleys, offering breathtaking views of the surrounding landscapes. The route also passes through several small towns, including Healdsburg and Sebastopol.

o **Yosemite National Park:** Yosemite National Park is a popular destination for motorcycle riders, offering several scenic routes through the park's unique landscape. The road winds through the park's mountains and offers stunning views of the surrounding valleys and mountains. The route also passes through several small towns, including Oakhurst and Mariposa.

o 91. **Trinity Alps:** The Trinity Alps are a popular destination for motorcycle riders, offering several scenic routes through the mountains' unique landscape. The road winds through the mountains and offers stunning views of the surrounding valleys and peaks. The route also passes through several small towns, including Weaverville and Hayfork.

o **Hollister to Pinnacles:** Overall, the route from Hollister to Pinnacles National Park offers motorcycle enthusiasts a scenic and enjoyable journey through the beautiful countryside of central California.

o **Mount Shasta:** Mount Shasta is a popular destination for motorcycle riders, offering several scenic routes through the mountain's unique landscape. The road winds through the mountain's forests and offers stunning views of the surrounding valleys and peaks. The route also passes through several small towns, including McCloud and Weed.

o **Lake Berryessa:** Lake Berryessa is a popular destination for motorcycle riders, offering several scenic routes through the Napa Valley. The road winds through the hills and offers stunning views of the surrounding vineyards and the lake. The route also passes through several small towns, including Napa and St. Helena.

o **Santa Cruz to Half Moon Bay:** This route takes riders along the beautiful coastline from Santa Cruz to Half Moon Bay. Half Moon Bay is known for its beaches, lighthouse, and charming downtown area. The road winds through the cliffs and offers stunning views of the Pacific Ocean and the surrounding landscape.

o **Mount Tamalpais:** Mount Tamalpais is a popular destination for motorcycle riders, offering several scenic routes through the mountain's unique landscape. The road winds through the mountain's forests and offers stunning views of the surrounding valleys and the city of San Francisco. The route also passes through several small towns, including Mill Valley and Fairfax.

# 5

# In the Southern California Area

o **Angeles Crest Highway:** Located in the San Gabriel Mountains, the Angeles Crest Highway is a popular motorcycle route that offers breathtaking views of the mountains and the surrounding forests. The way is over 60 miles long and features numerous twists and turns that are sure to thrill even the most experienced riders.

o **Death Valley:** While it may not be the most hospitable place on earth, Death Valley is a popular motorcycle destination for those looking for

o **Route 66:** Route 66 is one of the most famous motorcycle routes in the world, and it starts in Santa Monica, California. The route stretches for over 2,400 miles, taking riders through several states and offering a glimpse into the history of America. The California portion of Route 66 takes riders through the Mojave Desert and offers breathtaking views of the desert landscape.

o **Palm Springs:** Palm Springs is a popular destination for motorcycle riders, offering several scenic routes through the surrounding mountains and deserts. The road through Joshua

Tree National Park is a popular route, offering stunning views of the park's unique rock formations and desert landscape.

o**San Diego to Julian:** This route takes riders from the sunny beaches of San Diego to the charming mountain town of Julian. The road twists and turns through the mountains, offering stunning views of the surrounding valleys and forests. Julian is known for its apple pies, making it an excellent destination for a mid-ride snack

o**Route 1:** Route 1, also known as the Pacific Coast Highway, is one of the most iconic motorcycle routes in the world. The route takes riders along the California coast, offering breathtaking ocean views and the rugged coastline. The road features numerous twists and turns and steep climbs and descents, making it a challenging but rewarding ride.

o**Santa Monica Mountains:** The Santa Monica Mountains offer several scenic motorcycle routes that provide stunning views of the surrounding mountains and coastline. The Mulholland Highway is a popular route that offers over 20 miles of twists and turns, making it a challenging but rewarding ride. The Pacific Coast Highway is another popular route that takes riders along the coastline, offering breathtaking views of the ocean and the rugged coastline.

o**Big Bear Lake:** Big Bear Lake is a popular destination for motorcycle riders, offering several scenic routes through the San Bernardino Mountains. The road winds through the mountains and offers stunning views of the surrounding forests and valleys. The way also passes through several small towns, including Big Bear City and Fawnskin.

o **Joshua Tree National Park:** Joshua Tree National Park is a popular destination for motorcycle riders, offering several scenic routes through the park's unique rock formations and desert landscape. The Park features several twisting roads that offer stunning views of the surrounding mountains and valleys.

o **Twentynine Palms Highway,** this scenic route runs through the park's northern boundary and offers stunning views of the park's unique landscape. The Twentynine Palms Highway starts in the town of Twentynine Palms, just outside the park's Oasis Visitor Center. The road winds through the park's desert landscape, offering riders stunning views of the park's iconic Joshua trees, unique rock formations, and wide-open vistas. The route also passes through several small towns, including Joshua Tree and Yucca Valley.

o**San Gabriel Mountains:** The San Gabriel Mountains offer several scenic motorcycle routes that provide stunning views of the surrounding mountains and forests. The Angeles Crest Highway is a popular route that offers over 60 miles of twists and turns, making it a challenging but rewarding ride. Mount Baldy Road is another popular route that takes riders To the summit of Mount Baldy, offering stunning views of the surrounding valleys and mountains..

o **Salton Sea:** The Salton Sea is a popular destination for motorcycle riders, offering several scenic routes through the desert landscape. The road winds through the Salton Sea State Recreation Area, offering stunning views of the lake and the surrounding mountains. The route also passes through several small towns, including Niland and Mecca.

o **Los Angeles to Las Vegas:** This route takes riders from the bustling city of Los Angeles to the vibrant city of Las Vegas. The road winds through the Mojave Desert, offering stunning views of the surrounding mountains and valleys. The route also passes through several small towns, including Barstow and Baker.

o **San Diego County:** San Diego County is home to several scenic motorcycle routes offering stunning views of the mountains and coastline. The road winds through the county's hills and valleys, offering breathtaking views of the ocean and the surrounding landscapes. The route also passes through several small towns, including Julian and Ramona.

o **Death Valley National Park:** Death Valley National Park is a popular destination for motorcycle riders, offering several scenic routes through the park's unique landscape. The road winds through the park's mountains and valleys, offering stunning views of the surrounding sand dunes, canyons, and salt flats. The route also passes through several small towns, including Furnace Creek and Stovepipe Wells..

o **Sequoia and Kings Canyon National Parks:** Sequoia and Kings Canyon National Parks are popular destinations for motorcycle riders, offering several scenic routes through the parks' unique landscapes. The road winds through the park's forests and mountains, offering stunning views of the surrounding sequoia trees, canyons, and rivers. The route also passes through several small towns, including Three Rivers and Kings Canyon.

o **Santa Barbara County:** Santa Barbara County is home to several scenic motorcycle routes offering stunning views of the mountains and coastline. The road winds through the county's hills and valleys, offering breathtaking views of the ocean and the surrounding landscapes. The route also passes through several small towns, including Solvang and Santa Ynez.

o **Lompoc to Jalama Beach:** This route takes riders from the charming town of Lompoc to the secluded Jalama Beach. The road winds through the hills above the coastline, offering stunning views of the surrounding mountains and valleys. Jalama

Beach is a popular destination for surfers and beachgoers, making it an excellent place to relax after a ride.

o **Palomar Mountain:** Palomar Mountain is a popular destination for motorcycle riders, offering several scenic routes through the mountain's unique landscape. The road winds through the mountain's forests and offers stunning views of the surrounding valleys and hills. The route also passes through several small towns, including Pauma Valley and Lake Henshaw.

o **Tehachapi Loop:** The Tehachapi Loop is a popular motorcycle route that takes riders through the Tehachapi Mountains. The road features several twists and turns, as well as steep climbs and descents, making it a challenging but rewarding ride. The route also offers stunning views of the surrounding mountains and valleys.

o **Lake Arrowhead:** Lake Arrowhead is a popular destination for motorcycle riders, offering several scenic routes through the San Bernardino Mountains. The road winds through the mountains and offers stunning views of the surrounding forests and valleys. Lake Arrowhead is known for its crystal-clear waters, making it an excellent destination for a post-ride swim..

o **San Luis Obispo County:** San Luis Obispo County is home to several scenic motorcycle routes offering stunning views of the coastline and mountains. The road winds through the county's hills and valleys, offering breathtaking views of the ocean and the surrounding landscapes. The route also passes through several small towns, including Cambria and San Simeon..

o **Carrizo Plain National Monument:** Carrizo Plain National Monument is a popular destination for motorcycle riders, offering several scenic routes through the monument's unique landscape. The road winds through the monument's grasslands and offers stunning views of the surrounding mountains and valleys. The route also passes through several small towns, including Taft and Maricopa.

o **Death Valley Junction:** Death Valley Junction is a popular destination for motorcycle riders, offering several scenic routes through the desert landscape. The road winds through the Amargosa Desert and offers stunning views of the surrounding mountains and valleys. The route also passes through several small towns, including Shoshone and Tecopa.

o **Trabuco Canyon**: Trabuco Canyon is a beautiful Orange County, California. Start at the intersection of Santiago Canyon Road and Live Oak Canyon Road. As you ride through Trabuco Canyon, The road offers a mix of twists and turns, with plenty of opportunities to enjoy the thrill of the ride. Another highlight of the Trabuco Canyon ride is the Trabuco Oaks Steakhouse, a popular stop for riders looking to enjoy a meal or a drink in a rustic and charming setting.

o **Angeles Crest Highway:** Angeles Crest Highway is a popular destination for motorcycle riders, offering several scenic routes through the Angeles National Forest. The road winds through the forest and offers stunning views of the surrounding mountains and valleys. The way also passes through several small towns, including La Cañada Flintridge and Wrightwood.

o **Joshua Tree National Park:** Joshua Tree National Park is a popular destination for motorcycle riders, offering several scenic routes through the park's unique landscape. The road winds through the park's mountains and offers stunning views of the desert landscape. The route also passes through several small towns, including Twentynine Palms and Yucca Valley.

o **Inland Empire:** The Inland Empire region of California is home to several scenic motorcycle routes that offer stunning views of the surrounding mountains and valleys. The road winds through the region's hills and valleys, offering breath-taking views of the surrounding landscapes. The route also passes through several small towns, including Temecula and Lake Arrowhead..

o **Route 74:** Route 74 is a popular motorcycle route that takes riders through the Santa Ana Mountains. The road features numerous twists and turns and steep climbs and descents, making it a challenging but rewarding ride. The route also offers stunning views of the surrounding mountains and valleys.

o **Route 58:** Route 58 is a popular motorcycle route that takes riders through the Tehachapi Mountains. The road features numerous twists and turns and steep climbs and descents, making it a challenging but rewarding ride. The route also offers stunning views of the surrounding mountains and valleys.

o **Route 39:** Route 39 is a popular motorcycle route that takes riders through the San Gabriel Mountains. The road features numerous twists and turns and steep climbs and descents, making it a challenging but rewarding ride. The route also offers stunning views of the surrounding mountains and valleys.

o **Angeles Forest Highway:** Angeles Forest Highway is a popular destination for motorcycle riders, offering several scenic routes through the Angeles National Forest. The road winds through the forest and offers stunning views of the surrounding mountains and valleys. The route also passes through several small towns, including Valyermo and

Wrightwood.

o **Point Mugu:** Point Mugu is a popular destination for motorcycle riders, offering several scenic routes through the Santa Monica Mountains. The road winds through the mountains and offers stunning views of the surrounding coastline and cliffs. The route also passes through several small towns, including Malibu and Thousand Oaks.

o **Mount Wilson:** Mount Wilson is a popular destination for motorcycle riders, offering several scenic routes through the mountain's unique landscape. The road winds through the mountain's forests and offers stunning views of the surrounding valleys and the city of Los Angeles. The route also passes through several small towns, including Altadena and Pasadena.

o **Sequoia National Forest:** Sequoia National Forest is a popular destination for motorcycle riders, offering several scenic routes through the forest's unique landscape. The road winds through the woods and offers stunning views of the surrounding mountains and valleys. The route also passes through several small towns, including Kernville and Springville.

o **San Diego to Julian:** This route takes riders from the sunny city of San Diego to the charming mountain town of Julian. Julian is known for its delicious apple pies and its quaint downtown area. The road winds through the mountains and offers stunning views of the surrounding landscape.

o **Death Valley National Park:** Death Valley National Park is a popular destination for motorcycle riders, offering several scenic routes through the park's unique landscape. The road winds through the park's mountains and offers stunning views of the desert landscape. The route also passes through several small towns, including Shoshone and Furnace Creek.

o **Joshua Tree to Palm Springs:** This route takes riders from the unique landscape of Joshua Tree National Park to the desert oasis of Palm Springs. Palm Springs is known for its luxurious resorts, spas, and restaurants. The road winds through the desert and offers stunning views of the surrounding mountains and valleys.

o **San Luis Obispo to Hearst Castle:** This route takes riders along the beautiful Central Coast of California from the charming town of San Luis Obispo to Hearst Castle, the former residence of newspaper magnate William Randolph Hearst. The road winds through rolling hills and offers stunning views of the Pacific Ocean and the surrounding countryside.

o **Palomar Mountain:** Palomar Mountain is a popular destination for motorcycle riders, offering several scenic routes through the mountain's unique landscape. The road winds through the mountain's forests and offers stunning views of the surrounding valleys and mountains. The route also passes through several small towns, including Pauma Valley and Santa Ysabel.

o **Los Padres National Forest:** Los Padres National Forest is a popular destination for motorcycle riders, offering several scenic routes through the forest's unique landscape. The road winds through the forest and offers stunning views of the surrounding mountains and valleys. The route also passes through several small towns, including Ojai and Ventura.

o **Angeles Forest Scenic Byway:** Angeles Forest Scenic Byway is a popular destination for motorcycle riders, offering several scenic routes through the Angeles National Forest. The road winds through the forest and offers stunning views of the surrounding mountains and valleys. The route also passes through several small towns, including Palmdale and Acton.

6

# In the Central California Area

These are other areas that you will find that are worth exploring and fun riding to include in a trip

o **San Francisco to Lake Tahoe:** This route takes riders from the bustling city of San Francisco to the serene beauty of Lake Tahoe. The road winds through the Sierra Nevada Mountains, offering stunning views of the surrounding forests and mountains. Lake Tahoe is known for its crystal-clear waters, making it an excellent destination for a post-ride swim.

o **Central Coast:** The Central Coast of California is home to several scenic motorcycle routes that offer stunning views of the ocean and the coastline. The route takes riders through winding roads that pass through several charming coastal towns, including Santa Barbara, Morro Bay, and San Luis Obispo.

o **Eastern Sierra:**The Eastern Sierra region of California offers some of the most scenic motorcycle routes in the state.

o **San Francisco to Napa Valley:** This route takes riders from the bustling city of San Francisco to the serene surroundings of Napa Valley. The road winds through the hills above the town, offering stunning views of the surrounding landscape. Napa Valley is known for its vineyards and wineries, making it an excellent destination for wine lovers.

o **Mammoth Lakes:** Mammoth Lakes is a popular destination for motorcycle riders, offering several scenic routes through the Sierra Nevada Mountains. The road winds through the mountains and offers stunning views of the surrounding valleys and the Mammoth Lakes. The route also passes through several small towns, including June Lake and Lee Vining.

o **Lake Tahoe to Virginia City:** This route takes riders through the Sierra Nevada Mountains from Lake Tahoe to the historic mining town of Virginia City. Virginia City is known for its historic buildings and museums. The road winds through the mountains and offers stunning views of the surrounding valleys and peaks.

# 7

# In Conclusion

Throughout this article, we have covered many different regions and routes for motorcycle enthusiasts to explore in California. Some of the popular destinations include:

- The Pacific Coast Highway
- Napa Valley and Sonoma County
- Lake Tahoe and the Sierra Nevada Mountains
- Joshua Tree National Park and the Mojave Desert
- Big Sur and the Central Coast

Each region offers riders unique scenery, cultural experiences, and challenging routes.

While exploring California on a motorcycle can be an incredible experience, it's essential to prioritise safety and preparation. Riders should always wear appropriate safety gear, such as helmets and protective clothing, and ensure their motorcycle is in good working condition. They should also familiarise themselves with California's traffic laws and road regulations.

Finally, we encourage riders to take the time to explore

and experience the unique beauty and culture of Northern California on a motorcycle. Whether cruising along the Pacific Coast, winding through the mountains, or exploring small towns and vineyards, there's always something new to discover on two wheels. So get out there, explore, and ride safely!